IMAGES OF ENGLAND

Around Chard

Chard Town Hall, Fore Street, probably in the early 1920s. Originally known as the Corn Exchange and then the Guildhall, a clock tower was added to the Town Hall in 1834. The iron railings around the front vanished during a Second World War salvage drive. Complete refurbishment of the interior has recently been controversially completed.

IMAGES OF ENGLAND

Around Chard

Gerald Gosling
and
Frank Huddy

NONSUCH

Chard Grammar School, *c.* 1910. The school itself was founded in 1671 but was obviously in earlier (probably private) use because the date of 1538 appears on a leaden pipe there. Among its many pupils was Thomas Wakely, the medical and social reformer, and the founder and editor of The Lancet, who was born at Land Farm, Furley in 1795.

First published 2000
This new pocket edition 2005
Images unchanged from first edition

Nonsuch Publishing Limited
The Mill, Brimscombe Port,
Stroud, Gloucestershire, GL5 2QG
www.nonsuch-publishing.com

British Library Cataloguing in Publication Data.
A catalogue record for this book is available from the British Library.

ISBN 1-84588-138-9

Typesetting and origination by Nonsuch Publishing Limited
Printed in Great Britain by Oaklands Book Services Limited

Contents

Hughes & Co., seen here around the turn of the last century, were general drapers and milliners on the corner of High Street and Combe Street. In the early 1920s the building became Gill's Café and is today the Job Centre.

Introduction

'Change and decay in all around I see'

Chard may not have decayed, but it has been much changed from the Chard that I was born in when compared to the Chard that exists today. Everyone more or less knew everyone else, probably because it was a much smaller place than it is today. And it was a much livelier place as well. Every morning hundreds of people came into the town on buses from places as far away as Seaton, Lyme Regis, Crewkerne, Yeovil and Taunton, most of them to work in the factories that hummed with the noise of machinery and the talk of their workforce, many of whom went out into the town during their lunch hour to swell the already crowded streets. Local people shopped in the town and not in soulless supermarkets either on the edge of the town or out in the countryside itself. They shopped and gossiped and added to the air of industry the town gave out. There were more buses, more trains, two more stations and, until the last few sad years of Chard rail, great belches of steam and the shrill cry of the engine's whistle.

There were more pubs and, in proportion, less trouble, probably because there were far more policemen walking their beats on the street. There were delivery men bringing you your groceries, your daily bread, your weekend joint, your ice cream, your Corona drinks, your newspapers (Sunday, daily and evening), and much else besides. If it was needed for the everyday life of an everyday Chard family, it could be brought to your door.

Shops were much more personal, some of them even dark temples of a bygone age when everything from cheese and butter to tea and coffee was individually weighed and packaged at the rear of the premises. And, if you brought your own bottle, you got a halfpenny knocked off the price of a pint of vinegar that was drawn from a 5 gallon barrel in pint or half-pint measures. The greengrocer sold you veg that he knew came from the best growers in the district, the butcher bought his meat from the farmers he knew, and the fish was the best that the fishermen at Beer and Seaton could catch. Even the beer seemed stronger – it certainly tasted better. And there were the street stalls on market day, heaving with delicious produce, and the market itself with its noise from anxious cattle, sheep and pigs and, above them all, the raucous shout of the auctioneer. Above all, the farmers drove their cattle through the streets of Chard to that market and they worried not about the disruption to the traffic. After all they had been bringing their cattle into market that way since an age when talk of an invention such as an internal-combustion engine would have led to your becoming the star turn at a burning-at-the-stake production.

You paid for your purchase in pounds, shillings and pence, and there were 240 pennies in a pound because 240 of William the Conqueror's silver pennies were made from one pound of silver. Now it is 'new pees' and, over my dead body, may be even euros. You got your goods in ounces, pounds, hundredweights and even tons, good solid English tons, not metric tonnes, whatever they might be. Thankfully, cricketers still play on a 22-yard track and serious drinkers insist on beer in pints, but darts and football (could there be any more English games than that pair?) have gone foreign and we have incomprehensible measurements for the heights of goalposts and the length on an oche from the board.

Sadly, the Chard which had more noise and bustle as well as more time to sit and watch the others bustling, is gone for ever. Modern youth might point to such improvements as cars for all, TVs, washing machines, better health services, certainly more expectation of longevity, much more leisure time, more computers, more videos and an age when foreign travel is taken for granted. They could as well point to more crime, more intolerance, more reason to lock your doors at night, more need for more policemen and much more need for children not to speak to strangers.

My Chard has indeed gone for ever. Happily, for me and many others, Gerald Gosling and Frank Huddy have brought it all back with this wonderful collection of old pictures that brings much of that old Chard back for us all to share in.

Les Berry
July 2000

One

The Town

The Railway Hotel, East Street, c. 1904. Although built for the railway trade, the Railway Hotel continued as a pub after Dr Beeching's infamous axe put paid to both of Chard's stations. Since the closure of an inn on the Crewkerne Road of that name, the Railway Hotel has changed its name to the Happy Return, which would not have been an altogether unsuitable name for a railway hotel in the first place.

Snowdon Toll-House, *c.* 1910. One of the most photographed buildings in Somerset, the toll-house was constructed in 1839 by the Chard Turnpike Trust. Believe it or not, there was actually an upstairs room under the thatched roof, as a window in the rear will testify. The building was occupied until around the 1980s.

Stringfellow House, High Street, *c.* 1920. John Stringfellow was a Yorkshireman who moved to Chard in 1820 when he was twenty-one. It is said that he built a factory at the rear of this house but there are two schools of thought which are still debating whether this is true or not. What is certain is that Stringfellow produced his famous 'first powered-flight machine' from here and flew it at nearby Bewley Down. It has been said that the first flight took place in June 1848 in a mill in the town, but this has been the subject of some recent controversy. Stringfellow died aged eighty-four in 1883 and is buried in Chard cemetery in Crimchard where his grave may still be seen.

Although this 1935 Lillywhite postcard claims that this view is of the 'bottom of High Street, Chard', in actual fact it is taken well above the New Inn (on the left), which is now Chard Museum, placing it three-quarters of the way up High Street.

The Choughs Hotel, High Street, c. 1909. This fine old mullion-windowed building is said to have been the place where Judge Jeffreys stayed in 1683 and, after the Duke of Monmouth's ill-fated rebellion was crushed at Sedgemoor, sentenced twelve locals to be hanged. The sentence is supposed to have been carried out upon an oak tree that became known as Hangcross Tree.

Looking into Fore Street from High Street. Judging by the display of flags and bunting, the town has been decorated either for the Silver Jubilee of George V in 1935 or the Coronation of George VI in 1937. The tall building on the right was Chard's post office at the time.

Holyrood Street, c. 1908. The building in the centre rear was the London Inn which closed around the 1960s and became a Gateway's supermarket (now a branch of Somerfield's).

Holyrood Street in 1959, looking in the opposite direction to the picture at the foot of the page opposite. Parham & Sons in the background were general drapers, today there is a restaurant there. The small shop to its right would in the 1980s become the home of the Chard & Ilminster News, Chard's local paper and one that has faithfully chronicled its passing days ever since 1855.

Council School, Holyrood Street, c. 1918. In the wake of the many changes in the nation's educational system over the years, this school became Holyrood Senior School and is now known as Manor Court Primary School.

Boden's lace mill, Boden's Street, around 1905 when the claim was advanced, probably truthfully, that the town had a larger percentage of its inhabitants engaged in the manufacturing industries than any other town in England. The factory closed in 1938, and was sold and later became the home of Dualloys who were plain-bearing manufacturers. Today the building is mainly occupied by small industrial units.

Rose Terrace in Combe Street, c. 1924. On the right is the Phoenix Engineering Works who made (and still do) agricultural and industrial machinery, and export goods 'Made in Chard' to every corner of the globe.

Beasley's jewellery shop, Fore Street, c. 1902. It was once one of the longer-established businesses in Chard's main street and was still going strong sixty years later although it as now sadly closed. Seen in the doorway are George Beasley and his son Ernest.

Cambridge Street, c. 1900. Virtually unchanged a century later although Chard Town FC's Zembard Lane ground (see page 16) is now beyond the wall at the far end of the street. Surprisingly, there is no entrance to the ground at this point.

Combe Street around 1910 with Chard Cemetery House in the background. To the right of that house, but not visible in this picture, is Zembard Lane which leads to Chard Town FC's ground and, now, the new Holyrood School. Down the years there has been much controversy over the origin of the name of Zembard which many think derives from an old sand-pit that was once there.

Thatched houses at Crimchard, c. 1914. The houses on the left, but not the thatch, are still with us except for the one at the rear which was demolished and became the site of an industrial unit. In 1947 one half of the editorial team of this book actually worked there until the firm went bankrupt. The two facts are not connected!

The Old Manor House, Fore Street, c. 1911. Beyond it are the George Hotel and Frisby's shoe shop, both of which can be seen in the post-Second World War picture below. Sadly, however, the Frisby's chain no longer graces West Country towns.

The George Hotel, Fore Street, c. 1954. A famous old coaching inn with its stables still in existence at the rear, though no longer used as stables. The George recently closed and, after refurbishment, has reopened with the perhaps rather too apt name of the Phoenix.

Cornhill, Fore Street, around 1905, with the street market well in evidence. It is nice to know that, after many, many years absence, there is again a street market in Chard.

The Cornhill, twenty-five years after the picture above when, even if the buildings are not all that different, the main A30 road through the town has at last made its acquaintance with tarmac and a different kind of horsepower can be seen on the left.

The Guildhall, *c.* 1910. The picturesque and thatched Ball Inn to its left was still there in the 1970s. Sadly, however, it was demolished to make way for a branch of Messrs F.W. Woolworth's.

Fore Street, around 1951, at a time when the post-war boom in motor car ownership was becoming a problem, and one that was much increased on market days.

Above: A crowded Chard Market, 1907. Farmers from a wide area flocked to the town with their wives who did the week's shopping all at one go and the pubs did a roaring trade. After the Second World War the popularity of the market waned, due in no small way to the motor car having put the larger markets at Yeovil and Taunton, and even Exeter, well within reach. The auctioneers Messrs R. & C. Snell left Chard Market in 1954 and, despite a short spell when another firm of auctioneers tried to make a go of it, the market closed in 1955. *Below*: Part of the old market became Chard post office (now only a sorting office), the rest became the Fore Street car park seen here in the late 1990s.

Fore Street in 1970 with the Cerdic Cinema on the right. Chard once had two cinemas, the Regent being in High Street, but both are no longer with us. Today the Cerdic is a Weatherspoons public house and the Regent has been demolished, replaced by housing.

One of the dormitories at Chard School, 1940. A public school at the time, it even went as far as having the school's badge and foundation date (1671) on the blankets. Readers who served in the forces, either as a regular or during national service, will find the spartan washing bowl arrangements a trifle nostalgic.

The lower end of Fore Street, c. 1914.

Chard War Memorial Cottage Hospital. Seen here towards the end of the 1930s, it became a retirement home around 1981 and was then scheduled to become a residential dwelling.

An aerial view of Furnham church in the 1930s, although the postcard wrongly calls it Chard church. Chard School can be seen in the bottom left-hand corner.

Chard Central station, c. 1908. Chard was served by two stations, the Central Station was run by the GWR (Great Western Railway) and its line ran to Taunton, whereas Chard Town station, no more than a quarter of a mile away, connected the town to the L&SWR (London & South Western, later Southern, Railway) main Waterloo-Exeter line at Chard Junction. The two stations were connected. Chard Central was closed by Dr Beeching in 1966 but Chard Town, although closed to passenger traffic during the First World War (in 1917), carried goods traffic until the early 1970s when it was also closed.

Victoria Avenue, *c.* 1900. A little-photographed part of the town, Victoria Avenue looks much the same today. It was for many years the starting point for Chard carnival.

Furnham Road looking towards Chard in the 1930s. The main difference today is the considerable increase in motor traffic along the A358 which now takes traffic from the M5 to East Devon, West Dorset and, of course, Chard and its immediate vicinity.

THE RESERVOIR, CHARD.

Chard Reservoir was originally built to supply water for the Chard Canal which was opened in 1834 after many years of wrangling whether a canal could be built to connect Seaton, on the English Channel, with various spots on the Bristol Channel. In the end a canal was built as far as Chard that was capable of taking vessels up to 200 tons, but it came far too late and was never able to compete with the newly-arrived railway and closed in 1868. The fence in the picture runs along the edge of the railway line. The reservoir, seen here around 1899, is now a well-known wildlife reserve.

Opposite above: Fore Street, *c.* 1900. What appear to be gun carriages without their horses are parked in Fore Street, probably heading to or from army manœuvres.

Opposite below: Prospect House, Combe Street, *c.* 1910. This is the seldom-photographed home of James Gillingham (*c.* 1840-1924), the Chard-based shoe-maker and pioneer in artificial limbs.

Red Post Cross, between Wambrook and Chard, in the 1950s. So called because of the red signpost which this card mistakenly claims to be the only one in the country. Certainly one exists near Bere Regis in Dorset and there may well be others. Of more interest would be the question 'Why paint them red?'

Leigh House, near Chard, c. 1920. It was for many years the home of Sir Arthur Davies MP, but today, like so many fine old country buildings, it has been converted into residential flats.

Avishayes, between Chard and Chaffcombe, around 1918. It was recently purchased by Peter de Savery.

Chaffcombe village centre, *c.* 1925.

Combe Street and Crimchard around 1905 at the corner of Touchstone Lane (on the left) which, at the time, would have been almost too narrow for two carts to pass safely. Around 1970 the bottom end of Combe Street was blocked to north-bound traffic and Touchstone Lane was considerably widened and used as the main road to Combe St Nicholas and beyond.

Chaffcombe war memorial shortly after its dedication in 1921. Fourteen men are remembered here from the First World War and names of four from the Second World War were added later.

The International Stores, Fore Street, c. 1915. Once an important part of Chard's main shopping centre, the International Stores closed around 1960 and today the premises are broken up into smaller units.

E.H. Austin, Holyrood Street, c. 1906. E.H. Austin was a leading draper, milliner and men's outfitter's for Chard and a considerable part of the surrounding area of south-west Somerset. They actually had premises on both sides of the street which were still there seventy years later but both eventually closed. Like so many larger stores in small towns, these premises have been converted into smaller units.

Oaklands House, Crewkerne Road, c. 1895. A feature of the house was its observatory, a part of which can be seen behind the tall creeper-clad chimney at the front of the building.

Fore Street, c. 1905. Maybe not so crowded with traffic at the time of this picture, although there do appear to be more horse-drawn vehicles than normal in Chard's main thoroughfare. Of interest on the immediate left is a sign staying 'STOP' outside of the garage that, in later years, became a shop and was once the collection point for the Royal Blue and other coach firms. Possibly, in Edwardian Chard, it was used as a stopping place for coaches other than the Royal Mail which would have used Chard's main coaching hotel, the George. Chard was an important centre for the criss-cross carriers' routes that served the rural countryside away from the main coaching routes and it could well have been a stopping place for one or more of them.

Above: Looking down Fore Street towards the Guildhall (then called the Corn Exchange) around 1900. *Below:* Almost the same scene nearly a century later when much of the second-storey masonry has hardly been altered. Many old businesses whose names must have seemed as unchanging as the seasons to Edwardian, and later, Chardians have gone for ever.

Chard Museum, founded in 1970 at Godworthy House, High Street. Formerly the premises of the New Inn (one of some thirty public houses in Chard) which sadly closed around the 1960s. It will not be a great surprise to find that quite a large part of the museum is devoted to two of Chard's best-known names: John Stringfellow, the pioneer of powered flight, and James Gillingham, a pioneer in the field of artificial limbs. In recent years the museum has been the subject of considerable expansion and, in the last decade or so of the twentieth century, has received more than one award as an outstanding small museum.

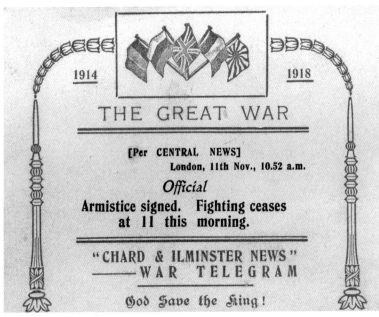

THE GREAT WAR

1914 1918

[Per CENTRAL NEWS]
London, 11th Nov., 10.52 a.m.

Official

**Armistice signed. Fighting ceases
at 11 this morning.**

"CHARD & ILMINSTER NEWS"
—— WAR TELEGRAM

God Save the King!

News that the fighting on the First World War, or 'The Great War' to the generation that fought it, had ceased and an Armistice signed, reached Chard through the offices of the *Chard & Illminster News* who had received the news through a Reuters News Agency telegram. The paper immediately produced this postcard, in patriotic red, white and blue colours, and the town itself half disappeared under a sea of flags and bunting. Most people sported red, white and blue rosettes and even some horses and dogs carried similar ribbons.

Lower High Street, *c.* 1909. The small building on the immediate right was the gatehouse for Mitchell Toms Ltd, the local brewers. Still there and, in view of its now being the subject of a preservation order, likely to stay there for all time. Sadly, however, the brewery behind has been converted into residential flats.

Two

At Work and Play

Haymaking at Chard, *c.* 1905. Modern mechanization has considerably reduced the workforce required to make hay, but, at the time, it was an occasion for work and much joviality and celebrations, usually, but not always, accompanied with ample supplies of good strong cider.

Above: The Chard fire engine attends a farm fire in 1905. The person second from the right is marked as 'captain' but no name is given. Few fires outside of the town failed to destroy the properties where they broke out. It was bound to take some time to reach Chard and raise the alarm, then the firemen had to assemble, harness the horses and make a journey of, on average, half an hour to reach the site of the outbreak. *Below:* The Chard fire brigade has been called to Peasemarsh Farm on 28 August 1906.

One of Mr Sully's earliest Dennis coaches that he began operating from the bottom of the town around the time of the First World War. In time the National Bus Co. reached Chard and, after a price war, Messrs Sully sold out to their rivals and went into the cinema business.

A Chard-bound Southern National coach about to leave the Castle Green bus station at Taunton around 1950. At the time Chard was an important stop on the Taunton-Seaton main bus route that connected towns on the Bristol and English Channels.

A 1908 view of the Snowdon Hill quarries where limestone and flint were worked. Robert Pope, whose name appears on the board of the wagon on the right, operated from these quarries and may well have been the owner.

Chard Rural District Council workmen engaged on road work near Chard. Of interest is the ubiquitous cider jar in the hands of the man on the extreme left.

A motorcycle press-ganged into use to crush linseed cake at a farm near Chard in the years before the First World War.

Workers at Gifford's (Holyrood) lace mills around the 1930s. Seated second from the right is Ruby Potter. The ladies seen here either had clean jobs or they have changed into party dresses for the occasion.

The Sully family were also in the haulage business, with Fred Sully working this Dennis lorry out of Whitestaunton, a hamlet to the west of Chard. Of interest in this picture, probably taken around 1919, are the solid tyres on the wheels.

Without wishing to make any suggestion, brewery workers always seem to be smiling! These seen at Messrs Brutton, Mitchell, Tom's brewery in High Street around 1950 certainly look cheerful. Among them are Mrs Burt, Roy Norcombe and Rene Jenkins.

The workforce of Phoenix Engineering Ltd outside their Combe Street factory around 1920.

Workers at Messrs F.J. Edwards Ltd pose before going on the factory's annual outing. They include Bob and Gordon Easton, Gordon Larcombe, Charlie Sutherley, Frank Penfold, Bob Trotter and Len Scriven, the coach driver.

An advertising card of the 1950s showing a milking parlour built by R.G. Spiller Ltd, building contractors in High Street, Chard, and with a branch at 10 Market Street, Crewkerne, where they were established in 1840.

Dening's carpenters and pattern-making shop, c. 1928. Reginald Long, in the white apron, was the foreman pattern-maker, who was also the president of the Chard & District Co-operative Society, and became mayor of Chard. Also in the picture are Fred Down, Bert Cornelius, Len Pring, Will Hoskins and Reg Hancock.

Above: Bert Reed inspecting seed drills just manufactured at Dening's factory in Crimchard in the 1950s. *Below*: A more modern seed drill is being checked in operation on a farm near Chard.

A Dening's straw baler waiting to be loaded in the goods bay at Chard Town station in 1950.

Dening's workforce outside the assembly shop around 1950.

A Dening's stand at an agricultural show, most likely the Royal Bath & West Show, around 1925. Charles Dening was originally a grocer in Chard. In the 1860s he joined forces with John Wightman of Lydmarsh to form an agricultural machinery manufacturing business in Old Town. At first known as Whightman and Dening, the firm changed its name to Dening & Co. and moved to Crimchard around 1881. The business stayed in the Dening family's hands until 1937 when it was sold but the name of Dening was retained in the trading title. Post-war financial troubles led to the firm becoming bankrupt around 1950.

A Chard workforce around 1906, although it is not known which factory this is. Two of the men appear to be wearing army uniforms.

The staff at Chard Town station around 1909. Chard Town was operated by the L&SWR and connected the town with their main Waterloo-Exeter line at Chard Junction.

Such was the volume of goods entering Chard and destined to be used at Wyatt's animal feed mills on Furnham Road, that they had their own siding connecting the factory with Chard Central station. Their silo can been be seen in the background of this 1950s picture.

Butter-making at the old dairy factory on the Chaffcombe Road near the reservoir around 1910. In later years the premises became Roger's Sunshine cider mills and are now, *sic transit gloria mundi* indeed, a council refuse dump.

Council-owned steamrollers preparing for work in the Chard area, probably in the 1920s when many of the rural roads of south-west Somerset were beginning to be introduced to the benefits of tarmac.

Chard Harmonic Society pose before a dress rehearsal in the Guildhall in 1909.

SUBSCRIBERS ONLY

CHARD MUNICIPAL BAND

Above: The bandsmen of the Chard Municipal Band outside the Chard Cricket Club pavilion in 1910. The band was a must for all civic and other occasions in the town and enjoyed a reputation far beyond the boundaries of the town. Below: Bank Holidays always found the band playing outside the Guildhall to a packed Fore Street seen here on Easter Sunday, 1912.

EASTER SUNDAY 1912

Left: Leonard Vere Preston was born at Ilminster in 1903, and went on to become Chard's most successful businessman, the secretary of Chard Agricultural Society, and clerk to the Chard Burial Board. He started his own accountancy firm and became an estate agent and substantial property owner in Chard after starting work for Canning & Kyrke, solicitors, for half-a-crown a week. His sporting life centred on the local Cotley Hunt and he followed local professional football with much interest. He died in 1994 at the age of ninety.

Below: Chard Church Lads' Brigade at a Dawlish camp in August 1909. Leonard Vere Preston is on the extreme right of the front row. The rather military and smart man behind him is Capt. Henry Bishop, and on the other end of that row is the padre, Father Owens of Furnham church.

Chard carnival seen leaving its Victoria Avenue marshalling area in 1907. Bradford's, the well-known Yeovil-based building and agricultural contractors, occupied the yard and buildings on the left at the time.

The visit of Bartlett's menagerie in 1906 coincided with Chard's carnival and they usually took part in the procession. Here the menagerie moves up Fore Street and passes the now demolished Congregational church on the left.

Chard's Edwardian carnivals aimed at raising cash for the local hospital and were usually held on Easter Saturday, such as this 1909 carnival procession in Fore Street as seen from the Guildhall balcony.

A 1930s Chard carnival queen and her entourage seen in Holyrood Street. Naturally 'royalty' needs protection, and it is provided here by one long arm of the Chard law.

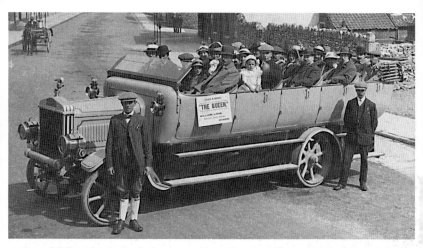

One of William Love's charabancs about to depart from his garage and stable in Holyrood Street in the early 1920s for an unknown destination, although Cheddar was a popular choice at the time. Charabancs were restricted to a 12mph speed limit and, with the solid tyres still in use at the time, it must have been a long, hard, tiring, and sometimes dusty journey. Imagine parking a vehicle at this angle in modern Holyrood Street!

Chard Town's A team pictured at their Zembard Lane ground in 1949/50. From left to right, back row: Charlie Old (manager), Bob Easton, F. Riley, Brian Beer, Bernard Trout, John Golesworthy, Bill Golesworthy, Dennis Stoodley. Front row: K. Sandland, Brian Mooney, Pete Hutter, Alan Brown, Mick Webber.

Chard sports ground at Dening Field, 1919. The open space in the foreground is the bowling green (now a car park) with the cricket club's thatched pavilion behind it.

Boden FC won the Perry Street & District League Championship for the first of what would be three successive seasons in 1908/09. They were the first Perry Street League side to reach the Somerset Junior Cup final (see opposite). The team members seen here are: ? Gregory, ? Dowell, ? Coles, ? House, Edgar Hancock, A. Follett and R. Follett, ? Miller, ? Pope, Ern Halse, and ? Kirby.

In 1912 Boden's became the first Perry Street & District League side ever to reach a county cup final when they met Clandown in the Somerset Junior Cup final at Street. Sadly they lost 4-1. Three weeks later their three-year reign as league champions was also ended. The players left Chard's Fore Street amidst tumultuous cries from supporters, and travelled to the game in the cars seen here and (maybe without cost) supplied by T. Press & Co., a well-known garage and coaching firm in the town.

Chard Homing Society, 1911. In the Edwardian years, and right down to the years immediately before the Second World War, pigeon racing was a well-supported sport in the town. Where this picture was taken is not known but, in all probability, it was some way from Chard in order to give the birds a decent race.

Lining up for a trotting race at Chard Sports and Races in 1906.

An unknown occasion outside Waterloo House in Fore Street around 1908 where a policeman is being decorated in front of what seems to be a military guard of honour. The townspeople of Chard and the town band are observing the ceremony.

Group 4, Holyrood Infants' School, Chard, c. 1907. Today Holyrood is known as Manor Court Infants' (Primary) School.

Chaffcombe celebrated the Coronation of George V in 1911 with a big tea party. Seen here is the committee that organized the event. This card, like many Chard views of the time, was produced by Montague Cooper, the well-known Somerset photographer who had studios at Chard, Bridgwater, Burnham-on-Sea, Taunton, Lynton and Wellington.

Chard Volunteer Band, c. 1900. The band is photographed outside the Victoria Hotel, on the junction of East Street and Victoria Avenue, before leading the Chard carnival procession. The two men on either side of the bandsmen are holding books with the title Chard Hospital Carnival – perhaps an account of the money raised by the carnival.

Chard town band, c. 1916. The band is still going and is now known as Chard Concert Band. Centre right is the mayor, Samuel Dening.

Above: Walking entries in the Chard carnival gather outside the Victoria Hotel prior to being judged. In the early years of the twentieth century Chard carnival was one of the highlights of the town's year and attracted huge crowds from far and wide. Called the Chard Hospital Carnival for many years, the profits went to Chard Hospital Comfort Funds. *Below:* The Sunday school walking entries are passing Norns Terrace in Furnham Road around 1900, presumably on their way to the judging in Victoria Avenue.

Chard Carnival, *c.* 1910. Above the procession passes the now-demolished Congregational Church (on left). The nearest float was entered by Coates and Company. A brush-making firm from Nimmer Mills, Wadeford. They enjoyed an international reputation, especially for their badger-hair shaving brushes. This picture, and the one below, were taken from the balcony of the Guildhall.

The caption on this postcard says, 'Mlle Florence walking on the Ball at Chard on 8 March 1907.' She can be seen on the right surrounded by an admiring and curious crowd of Chardians outside the George Hotel.

St Mary's Church School treat, 1911. Of interest is the fact that this card, addressed to Miss E. Brown, 7 Crimchard, Chard, was posted at 9.45 a.m. and bears the message, 'I shall be up tonight at 7.20'. In those days all mail was ultra first-class and, it seems, one could arrange one's dates at the last moment without any worries about the lady not turning up – unless she no longer fancied you!

In 1911 King George V Coronation mugs were presented to all Chard schoolchildren by Mayor Samuel Henry Dening. This mug turned up in Carmarthen Market in the early 1990s when it was bought for £10.

Samuel Henry Dening presenting the mugs to the children of Chard. He is standing in front of a table covered with mugs and, judging by the other gentleman on the left, needed some help in the actual presentation.

Above: Gen. Booth, the founder of the Salvation Army, seen addressing a crowd outside the Guildhall in 1906. It was the custom for Gen. Booth to halt outside the town he was visiting and sit in his car while it was drawn into the town centre by ropes. Although one might think that if he came from the Honiton direction the men had an easy downhill pull, here the cars are pointing up Fore Street which suggests they had a hard uphill pull instead. *Below:* A crowd gathers outside the Guildhall for a now-unknown civic occasion. The postcard bears a January 1924 postmark but the presence of Samuel Henry Dening with his mayoral chains suggests an even earlier date than that.

A rare picture indeed: Group 1, Southend IC School, Chard, around 1905. The Southend School was situated on the southern outskirts of the town on the Axminster Road, hence the name, and has long since ceased to be a school. It was used a troops' billet in the Second World War, was once a pencil factory and is now a residential mews.

Chard Observer Corps on parade during the Second World War. From left to right, back row: 'Rubberneck' Jennings, Archie Long, -?-, -?-, -?-, -?-, 'Monkey' Fear (a well-known jeweller in Holyrood Street). Front row: Fred Culverwell, Mr Benham, Mr Evans (manager of the Phoenix Engineering factory), -?-, Ernest Ashman (headmaster of Holyrood School), Frank O'Dare, Mr Ling, -?-.

Chard brewers Mitchell, Toms & Co. Ltd were founded in 1771 as they proudly claim on their float in the trade section of the 1925 Chard carnival. Their brewery in High Street was in use until the 1970s and is now residential flats. Mitchell, Toms amalgamated with the Brutton brewery and in time became part of the Bass empire.

The Chard branch-line train affectionately, if rudely, called the 'Chard Snail', was derailed near Creech St Michael around 1906.

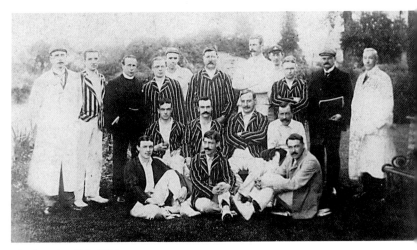

Chard Cricket Club, 1904.

The Yuletide Bazaar in the Guildhall, seen here in 1913, was always a great attraction and most of Chard paid to go inside and look out for last minute Christmas presents.

The Chard Quadrille Band (Lovell Brothers) at a function in the Guildhall in the 1920s.

The Tony Graham Combo dance band in 1962. From left to right: Graham Windsor, Frank Huddy, Mo Cunnold, Jack Newhouse, Tony Burt. The band was formed in 1959 and was a popular attraction throughout the south, south-west and South Wales for some twenty-five years. One of their more memorable occasions was the dance held to mark the scrapping of the Ark Royal at Plymouth where they played in front of over 2000 people.

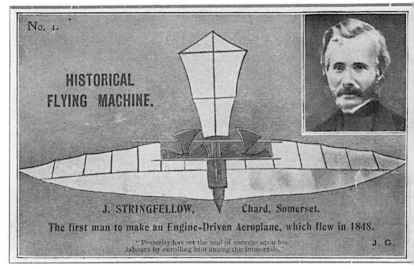

No. 1.

HISTORICAL
FLYING MACHINE.

J. STRINGFELLOW, Chard, Somerset.

The first man to make an Engine-Driven Aeroplane, which flew in 1848.

"Posterity has set the seal of success upon his labours by enrolling him among the immortals."

J. G.

Above: John Stringfellow was the first man to make an engine-driven aeroplane when he flew his model on Bewley Down (see page 10). *Below:* A later aviation pioneer to visit Chard was the Frenchman Salmet who gave a flying display outside the town on 30 May 1912. He is seen here, wearing goggles, with Mayor Samuel Dening on his left. On Mr Dening's left is James Gillingham, the Chard-based pioneer of artificial limbs, most of which he designed himself at his workshop in Combe Street where he worked for sixty years.

M. SALMET. HIS WORSHIP THE MAYOR & MR GILLINGHAM
CHARD MAY 30TH 1912

This picture is a fake. The occasion is the visit of the French aviator Salmet (see opposite) but as the crowd is not the least bit interested in the aeroplane overhead, it has obviously been added later by the photographer. The photography of the time would not have produced such a clear image of a quickly moving object.

A modern group of Chardians with a model of Stringfellow's aeroplane with Furnham church in the background.

The whole of Victoria Avenue poses at the Furnham Church Rooms on 20 November 1947 to mark the wedding of Princess Elizabeth (now Queen Elizabeth II) to Prince Philip Mountbatten. Among those present are Ray Larcombe, Brian Cooke, Clarence Harvey, Sandra Larcombe, Maurice Bandy, Mrs Larcombe, Mrs Harvey, Mrs De Pledge, Audrey De Pledge, Mrs Cooke, Mrs Hodges, Lawrence Hodges, Mrs Daniels and June Larcombe.

Holyrood School's production of *Iolanthe* in 1955 which was directed by Mr Coleman. Among those seen here are Beatrix Peadon, Robert White, Janet Cunnold, Mavis Martin, Jean Rowley, Christine Kilby, Peter Gage, Bob Chick, Neil Gollop, Valerie Dabinett, Brian Cooke and Joy Everett.

Right: Tatworth School's under nines team became the South West Under Nines Football Champions in 1977.

Below: The annual concert at High Street School, Chard in 1951. The pupils include Madeline Pring, Sue Hopkins, Adrian Phippen, Clarence Harvey, Brian Cooke, Robin Lilley, Brenda Smith, Derek Redpath, Peter Howard, Philip Brown, Tony Page, Alan Case, Douglas Morgan and Raymond Chick.

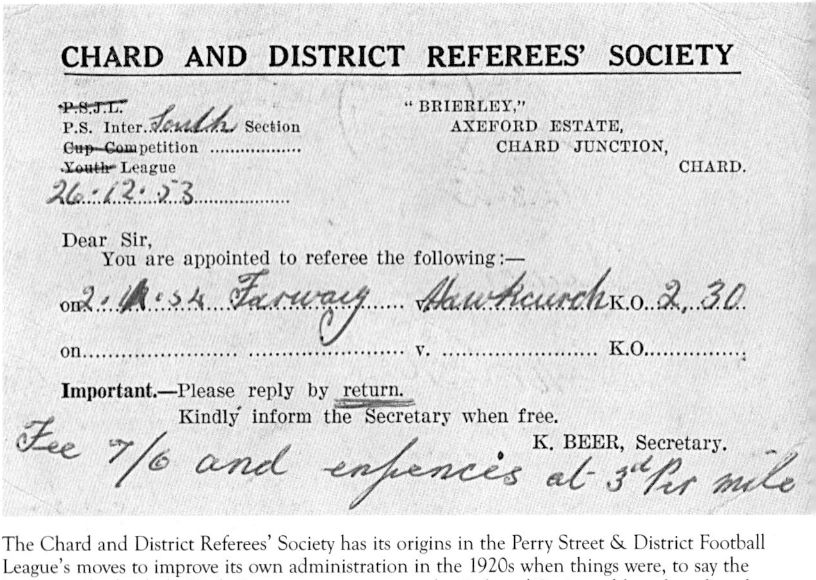

CHARD AND DISTRICT REFEREES' SOCIETY

P.S.J.L.
P.S. Inter. *South* Section
Cup Competition ....
Youth League
26. 12. 53

" BRIERLEY,"
AXEFORD ESTATE,
CHARD JUNCTION,
CHARD.

Dear Sir,
    You are appointed to referee the following :—
on 2. 1. 54 *Farway* *Hawkchurch* K.O. 2. 30

on.................................. v. .... K.O...............;

Important.—Please reply by <u>return</u>.
        Kindly inform the Secretary when free.
                                K. BEER, Secretary.

Fee 7/6 and expences at 3ᵈ per mile

The Chard and District Referees' Society has its origins in the Perry Street & District Football League's moves to improve its own administration in the 1920s when things were, to say the least, a trifle slapdash. With the improvement came the Referees' Society, although at first they were merely an offshoot of the league's management committee. The society is still strong in local football. Seen here is an appointment card sending referee Reg Watts of Honiton to an Intermediate South match between Farway and Hawkchurch. Mr Watts received 7s 6d for his trouble – plus 3d a mile travel expenses!

BODENS V HOLYROOD MILLS

Boden's & Co. *v.* Holyrood Mills in a Perry Street & District Football League game around 1908 and during Boden's three-year reign as champions. At the end of the 1905/06 season Holyrood Mills went to Axminster to play their last match at a time when the losers of the game would finish bottom. When they went out on to the field they found that some wag had tied a wooden spoon with yellow and blue ribbons (their colours) to a goalpost. They had the last laugh, however. They won and Axminster finished bottom!

Holyrood Mills football team in the 1912/13 season when they finished seventh (out of nine teams) in the Perry Street & District League. Their ground was in Union Lane and said to be one of the best in the district. The players in this photograph are, from left to right, back row: A. Pinney, Joe Dampier, J. Hockey. Middle row: E. Jewell, V. Cook, G. Kerle. Front row: F. White, W. Beaviss, Tommy Kerle, W. Stacey, W. Long.

Holyrood Mills Reserves, 1911/12. At the time the second team only played friendly games but after the First World War when the Perry Street & District League ran an Intermediate Section they played league football for a short spell. In this picture, as was the custom at the time, the players have lined up for their photograph in team formation. The back row is right-back, keeper, left-back; the middle row is right-half, centre-half and left-half; and the front row is right-wing, inside right, centre forward, inside left and left-wing.

Above: The All Blacks *v.* the All Whites, probably at Boden's ground in Union Lane, Chard, in 1906. The mayor of Chard kicked-off and of special interest is the kit worn by the referee which is suspiciously like his Sunday best. What the occasion was is not now known but, at that time, the Chard Mill teams played a friendly with the rest of the Perry Street League clubs to raise money for league funds. *Below:* The Chard Volunteer football team on 20 April 1918. Made up of local soldiers, they never actually played league football after the end of the First World War, but, for a short spell, there was a Chard Comrades team, a forerunner of the British (now Royal British) Legion.

Boden & Co. *v.* Combe Rovers around 1911. By the time of the picture Combe Rovers were no longer the force of their early years when they were renowned for their robust outlook on the game. It is said that their motto could have been, 'If it moved kick it. If it didn't move, kick it to make it move'.

Chard Girl Guides in the 1920s.

CHARD TOWN FOOTBALL CLUB

Souvenir Programme

THURSDAY, APRIL 27
—
CHARD TOWN
v.
BRISTOL CITY
KICK-OFF
6.30 p.m.

This Programme is issued by the Chard Town
Association Football Club Supporters' Club

Price: THREEPENCE

Left: Although this programme bears the date 27 April, it omits the year. Judging by the Chard team inside, however, Charlie Smith, Diddle Fowler, Bernard Bush, Ron Amos, Bill Wyatt, Denny Harrison, Ken Miller, Tommy Charles, Ginger Cox, Don Harris and Lionel Hodge, it must have been in the early 1950s. Chard Town had a connection with Bristol City because Mike Thresher was signed from Chard by City manager Pat Beasley who later became manager at Chard.

Below: A trade entry at Chard Show around 1906.

Chard Band in 1905 playing at what appears to be a rugby ground, although the posts in the background seem to be of a makeshift nature.

GOOD SHEPHERD 1909

The ladies of the Church of the Good Shepherd in 1909. As would only be expected of the Edwardian fair sex, a magnificent (and there can be no other word) array of Sunday best hats are on show.

A donkey derby at Chard Horse Show and Races around 1905.

Another good show of hats, if not quite as magnificent as those on the previous page. Who these ladies are and what their destination is are not known, but the dress places the occasion around 1930.

Chard Cricket Club on their Dening Field ground, 1928. From left to right, back row: -?-, -?-, Bert Scott, Harold Gollop, Cyril Golesworthy, -?-, ? Gillingham, Don Golesworthy, -?-,-?-. Middle row: 'Nesty' Dening, Mr Inge, Bertie Dening. Front row: -?-, A. Larcombe, Arthur Larcombe, H. Larcombe.

C.U.F.C., 1910/11. One of many teams in Chard during Edwardian times that only played friendly games, C.U.F.C. could be Chard United or even the Conservative & Unionist FC, after all, the local Tories did run a successful cricket team for many years and there was a Conservative AFC in Chard in 1906 (see page 83). If it was Chard United, the name resurfaced in the 1970s when a team of that name was formed and joined the Perry Street & District Football League.

Probably not a Chard carnival procession, as there are not enough spectators, but more likely a church or chapel treat going to the railway station. Here they are turning into Victoria Avenue from East Street around 1905.

Right: The Exchange Cinema, Chard, with a card advertising a film starring Mrs Vernon Castle for two nights, Friday and Saturday, 25 and 26 January. The Exchange Cinema was in the Corn Exchange (now the Guildhall) and was a forerunner of Chard's two cinemas – the Regent and the Cerdic, both of which are no longer cinemas.

EXCHANGE CINEMA, CHARD
- Fridays and Saturdays -
Commencing January 25 & 26

Below: Chard Conservative AFC, 1906. It is not known now where the Tories played or for how long they were in existence. They certainly did not play in any local league and, in the absence of any town or village rivalry, one can only assume that their local derby game was when they played the Liberals.

CONSERVATIVE A.F.C. CHARD.1906.

Chard British Legion (now the Royal British Legion) pictured on the town's Dening Field cricket ground around 1932. No record of the names of those present exist, nor for what occasion they have gathered.

Three

Tatworth and South Chard

Packing-room staff at Wilts United Dairy at Chard Junction around 1957. Among those present are Violet Martin, Joe Crook, Peggy Froom and Joyce Male.

Tatworth church choir outing, 1928. It was almost compulsory for all charabanc outings to Cheddar Gorge to be photographed outside Gough's Cave. Among those here are Ben Walden, Bob Huddy, Henry Summers and Gilbert Huddy.

Office staff at Wilts United Dairy around 1950. From left to right: -?-, Yvonne Webber, Ruby Morris, -?-, -?-, Barbara Heal.

Tatworth Infants' School Christmas party, *c.* 1948. Among the children present are Jean Martin, Diane Tomerson, Andrew Culverwell, Alan Board, Trevor Symes, Glenys Down, Rex Bowditch, Jill Hayball, Patsy Andrew, David Jerrett, Jean Lacey, Enice Scott, Marion Sweetland, Joy Everett, Jean Hurford, Robert Davies, David Wallace, Pat Bilyard, Robert Hawker, Richard Hawker. The helpers include: Gerald Quick, Vera Sweetland, Bob Pallister, Charlie Hodges, Aubrey Searle, Nora Searle and Mrs Best.

Perry Street & Yonder Hill FC in the 1925/26 season when they won the Perry Street League Charity Cup, beating Beer Albion 5-4 in a nine-goal thriller final, and the Lyme Hospital Cup where they beat Bridport 5-0 in the final on Lyme's old Sidmouth Road ground. Before the First World War there was a Perry Street Works FC and also a Yonder Hill FC, both playing in the Perry Street & District League. The works team folded in 1920 and a village side was formed which amalgamated with the old Yonder Hill team and, apart from a couple of seasons, has been a member of the Perry Street & District League ever since. From left to right, back row: L.E. Folman, H. Woolcott, L. Hallett, C. Harris, C. Churchill, H Warne, A.T. Wells (secretary). Middle row: F. Bodger, E. Brewer, Len Chambers (chairman), A. Larcombe, T. White, R. Best (trainer). Front row: W.D. White, L. Churchill, G. Meech, G. Barratt, L.H. 'Lusty' Brewer, F.S. Bilyard.

Chard Road Hotel, Chard Junction, 1906. The hotel was built around 1859 to cater for the railway traffic that the recently constructed Chard Junction brought. It survived Beeching, became known as the Three Counties Hotel and is now a private residence.

The butter factory of Wilts United Dairies Ltd at Chard Junction in the 1950s. Badly bombed, with one fatal casualty, during the Second World War, the factory made national newspaper headlines in 1958 when it set up a now surpassed world record production of 104 tons of butter in one day.

Perry Street House at South Chard, seen here around 1938, was once the home of Charles Small, the owner of Perry Street lace works (now Swiss Net Ltd) and the founder of the Perry Street & District League. He was a man of much substance and, in the manner of such men, was on the Chard School Board of Governors, the Chard Rural District Council, a chairman of Chard Parish Council and a school manager. In 1916 he married Miss Elsie Dening, the daughter of Samuel Henry Dening, a member of the engineering family that had its factory at Crimchard. Charles Small died on 2 February 1919, aged forty-five, a victim of the post-war influenza epidemic. All the factories in Chard closed during the hour of his interment.

Perry Street Works FC in the 1905/06 season when they won the Perry Street & District
Football League. From left to right, back row: George Holman (secretary), C. Hodges, George
Lee, G. Hussey, Charles Small (president). Middle row: George Stokes, A. Holman, O. Legg,
J. Heal, Henry Willey. Front row: Fred Wheaton, Fred Hoskins, Len Chambers, T. Bowditch,
C. Morris. Two secretaries of the Perry Street & District League are in this team photograph:
Henry Willey was the league's first secretary and served from 1903 until 1919, and Fred
Wheaton served after that and also stood in as treasurer for a spell. The story is often told that
Charles Small, a keen sportsman with special interest in cricket and football, wanted to start a
local league and told Henry Willey, one of his employees, 'We are going to have a league and
you are going to be the secretary'.

Timber hauling for Yonder Hill sawmills, 1931. The two men are seen working the lifting jack by means of which the front end of the butt is being pushed over towards the near side of the trailer so that it will rest centrally on the timber carriage. On the reverse of the card someone has written that this was 'an example of the mastery of brain and mechanical appliances over mere inert mass'.

Above: Fun and games with skittling for a pig at Chard Common sports in 1955. Helen Meech (*née* Board) throws the first ball. As a butcher's daughter, a pig would have been a useful prize if she had won it. Watching Helen are her husband Geoff Meech, June Froom, Joan Tomerson, Kingsley Collins and Harry Stonham.

Right: Felling the famous Tatworth Tree around 1969 to make way for road improvements on a busy junction outside Tatworth parish church. The fir tree was planted in 1887 to mark Queen Victoria's Golden Jubilee. Not unexpectedly the parishioners mounted a fierce campaign to save their tree, a meeting place for everyone in the village from courting couples to those who just wanted a good gossip. But even a petition to HM Government failed to save it and it was lopped and then felled in front of a huge crowd who heckled and shouted incessantly throughout the operation.

Above: E.M. Board & Son's Tatworth butchers shop, *c.* 1959. The business was started by George Board, and was continued after his death by his widow Edith Matilda. Their son Frederick William then ran the shop and was followed in turn by his children, Helen, John and Alan (in the picture). The business is still in the family's hands. *Below:* The Board's friendly rival, Vandyke Purse (first left) the South Chard butcher, casting an eye over some prize cattle at Hay Farm, Winsham, around 1949. With Mr Purse are Sid Dommett, Albert Graham and Bill Moore.

An outing to Weymouth for the youth club at Tatworth in 1948. From left to right, back row: John Hoare, Mike Bowditch, Lester Bishop, Jack Ellis. Front row: -?-, Barbara Heal, Arthur Sharp, Alec Chambers, Audrey Haines, Len Bond, Mary Hallett, -?-.

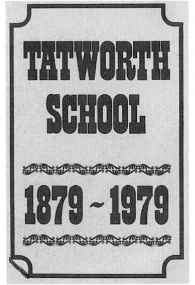

TATWORTH SCHOOL

1879 ~ 1979

Above: Tatworth School, 1910. The school was founded in 1879 under Chard School Board and opened by Revd Preb. Buller, vicar of Chard. The first headmaster was Mr T. Browne and the infants' teacher was Miss Ada Mitton and between them they taught around 100 children, a third of whom, according to the school logbook, did not know their alphabet. This building was recently demolished and has been replaced by a modern school.

Left: The programme for the celebrations for Tatworth School's centenary in 1979.

Tatworth School infants' class, 1906. It was around this time that Fred Bonfield, a pupil at the school, received a medal for six years' unbroken attendance which, given the epidemics that swept most schools at the time, was more than unusual.

A Christmas concert at Tatworth Primary School around 1979.

Jesse Brewer, the landlord of the Golden Fleece at Chard Common, Tatworth, pictured in the inn's doorway around 1930. The pub was closed for some eighteen months and has recently reopened as a freehouse in June 2000.

Vandyke Purse's butchers shop in South Chard.

Dyke Hill, Perry Street, around 1950, although the postcard says 'South Chard'. Where Perry Street, South Chard and, indeed, Tatworth begin and end is a source of much puzzlement to the casual passer-by and, although there might well be an outcry from the other two constituents, surely there is a need for a combined parish of Tatworth, or South Chard, or Perry Street?

The church of St John the Evangelist at Tatworth around 1920, with the Tatworth Tree on the left. A pleasing part of the Armistice Day service (now Remembrance Sunday) at the church was the laying of a wreath on behalf of the Perry Street & District Football League by Mrs Elsie Small, its president and the widow of the founder, Charles Small, who is remembered by a wall-plaque inside the church. Sadly the wreath-laying by the league seems to have died out after the Second World War.

An Edwardian wedding that joined two well-known Tatworth families. In front are Frank Hawker and his bride, Dora Hayball, and behind them are the best man, Henry Dening, and bridesmaid Lillian Hayball. Frank and Dora's grandchildren and great-grandchildren still live in the village.

Gulwell Cottage, South Chard, c. 1965. This charming old house, which attracts many a photographer, is near the church of St John the Evangelist and was for many years run as a restaurant and guest house by Mr and Mrs Wilson. Today it has again reverted to private use.

Parrock's Lodge in Tatworth, despite the caption on this 1901 postcard which puts it in Chard. The home of the Langdon family for many years and occupied by nine Langdon children, none of whom married, it is now residential flats, although the top storey was demolished in the 1960s.

Chard Junction around 1960 showing the Chard branch-line on the left and the Chard Road Hotel (see p. 89) in the background.

Chard Junction, c. 1960. The junction was opened on 19 July 1860, not all that long before the completion of the Exeter extension of the Waterloo-Salisbury line.

Dyke Hill, Tatworth, enjoying a quiet, traffic-free, summer's day in 1960. Today, of course, the road is in constant use by traffic, especially the heavy tankers from the dairy at Chard Junction.

The same spot at the same time as the picture above but looking towards Axminster instead of Crewkerne.

School Lane, South Chard, around 1960, with the now demolished Tatworth Primary School in the background.

The old blacksmith's forge in School Lane, South Chard, around 1960. Sadly this handsome house has lost its top storey.

St Margaret's chapel, South Chard, 1909. The chapel was once connected with the Church of England as a chapel of ease to St Mary's parish church in Chard. It is one of the oldest buildings in the village having been a private house during the time of the Commonwealth when it was owned by a Mr Deane, a member of a very old Tatworth family, and was mentioned in his will. The walls are 3ft thick in places. In 1895 it was repaired, much altered inside and reseated throughout, but by 1914 it was thought to be unsafe and fell into a state of disuse until the Second World War when it was used as a classroom for evacuated children from London's East End. It has been made safe again and is now a private dwelling.

The Baptist following in South Chard moved across the road from the old St Margaret's church to a new chapel in 1909 and they are seen here at the foundation-stone laying ceremony on 9 April that year.

The opening ceremony of Tatworth School swimming pool in 1966. From left to right: Revd Coleridge (a descendent of Samuel Taylor Coleridge who was born at nearby Ottery St Mary), Lloyd Staples (chairman of the Board of Governors), -?-, Mr Weekes (headmaster).

Right: Geoff and Helen Meech with Celia Sturdy, a customer's daughter, outside the Board family butcher's shop at Chard Junction in the mid-1960s (see p. 94).

Below: Colin Hounsell astride his motorcycle in Tatworth around 1922. Note the solid tyres, carbide lamps and the large flywheel that powered the rear wheel.

Left: Mary Summers pictured outside her family's home in Tatworth Street around 1930.

Below: The post office, South Chard, *c.* 1965. The post office was run by the Misses Thorne from a small room (its window is to the left of the porch) in the house on the right. The post office moved into the premises seen here around 1960 and, despite a decline in the numbers of small rural post offices, is still open today. Back in the 1880s South Chard had only a receiving house run by Thomas Spurdle. A receiving house was what the name suggests: a place, a private house, shop, or even a pub, where mail was received from customers for the postman to collect and take to Chard. In this instance the mail was collected at 6.15 p.m. every evening except Sundays.

The Post Office, South Chard   No. 7181

Cricket House, Cricket St Thomas, near Tatworth, c. 1925. Famous in later years, of course, as a theme park with Noel Edmunds connections, and the setting for the popular TV series *To The Manor Born*. Today, after a £20 million conversion, it is a flagship of the Warner empire.

An outing for Tatworth parishioners to Weymouth in 1951. Among those seen here are Mrs Galpin, Mrs Heal, Mrs House, Mrs Scott and Tom White.

YE OLDE POPPE INNE, NR. CHARD.

44611

Tatworth Primary School around 1928 when their class-room was decked out as a village grocery shop. Violet Owen is the young girl in white in the middle with Les Moss on her left. They became childhood sweethearts and were later married for over fifty years. Presumably all the goods were borrowed from a real shop and it would all fetch a handsome sum from an antique dealer today.

Opposite above: The big freeze-up of the winter of 1962–1963 was just another obstacle to be overcome by the countryside delivery-men who are well versed in keeping going come snow, hail or whatever. Here Co-op milkman Harold Grabham, seen near Tatworth, needed assistance from four comrades to get the milk to outlying areas. Harold is kneeling in front of his float and among the helpers are Phil Barnes, Gordon Coles and Vic Collins. The fourth person was an unknown passer-by who was press-ganged into helping.

Opposite below: The Poppe Inn, Tatworth, 1956. Little changed apart from the front door which is no longer in use because of the danger from the considerable increase in traffic on the Chard-Axminster road that runs past the inn.

Above: Tatworth School maypole dancing class, 1909.

Left: Tatworth School's netball team became the South West Somerset Under Elevens Netball Champtions in 1977.

Four

Combe St Nicholas
and Chardstock

A trick picture of Combe St Nicholas around 1903 which has been printed in reverse.

Combe St Nicholas School, 1928. From left to right, back row: William Hill, Ron Hake, Cyril Ward, Jack Symes, Sid Scriven, Ray Bailey, Gupp Player, Len Trott, -?-, Reg Hutchings. Second row: -?-, Vera Symes, -?-, Edie Fowler, Lillian Bartlett, Renee Slade, -?-, -?-, Edie Graham, -?-, -?-. Third row: -?-, Edie Long, Stella Miles, Hilda Eastwood, Edna Scriven, Nora Collins, -?-, Agnes Hocken, Florrie Hopkins, -?-, -?-. Front row: Herbert Rideout, George Duck, -?-, Charles Symes, Jack Venn, Billy Huish, -?-, Cyril Mear, Jack Aplin, Tony Trott, Harry Owsley. The headteacher, Mr Wheaton, is on the right, and his assistant Mr Jarvis is on the left.

Above: Wesleyan Sunday school children enjoy their annual treat at Combe St Nicholas in June 1907. *Below:* The children march in procession through the village behind the Crewkerne Salvation Army Band under bandmaster Barrett to the Weslyan chapel where a special service was conducted by the Revd A.M. Chirgwin of Ilminster. There were about 120 children present and as many as 150 parents and friends all of whom sat down to a huge tea and enjoyed games, swings and races. Two long arms of the Combe law keep a friendly eye on events, one of them conveniently placed outside the George Inn which, sadly, is now three private dwellings.

Above: The Green, Combe St Nicholas, c. 1962. *Below:* The George Inn during the same period. At that time the landlord was Jack Venn who played football for Combe St Nicholas in the 1930s when he acted as secretary for the club. The village football club disbanded when he had to stand down around 1937, and did not start up again until the 1960s when the secretary was, again, Jack Venn.

Combe St Nicholas post office, with the chapel in the background, c. 1935.

The Rising Sun, Wadeford, between Combe St Nicholas and Chard, c. 1900. The licensee at the time was John Player but it is not known if he is one of the two men in the picture.

An unusual view from The Green at Combe St Nicholas around 1899 showing Shira Cottage to the left of the post office. Tythe Cottage is the thatched building in the background with the roof of the rectory peeping out from behind it. The Rectory was converted into flats in the 1970s.

Looking down the rather grandly called Village High Street around 1899 with the George Inn on the left. Behind the trees on the right is St Nicholas' parish church, a particularly fine building. It is surprising, apart from the George and the trees, how little change there has been in this view over the succeeding 100 years.

Combe St Nicholas School football team, 1921. From left to right, back row: Leonard Bailey (linesman), Martyn Hocken, -?-, Mr Schofield, Mr Fred Wheaton, -?-, -?-. Front row: Jesse Jeffery, Leslie Venn, Ernie Mear, Harold Froom, C. Cleal, F. Player, -?-. Seated: -?-, Bert Bartlett. Fred Wheaton, the school's headmaster, was a former player with Perry Street Works FC, and played in their Perry Street & District League Championship side in 1905 (see page 91). He is buried in Combe church where a plaque on the tower screen states, 'To the Glory of God and in Memory of Frederick Henry Wheaton. Born December 2nd 1895, died February 12th 1938. For 22 years schoolmaster of this parish and associated with the administration of the Perry Street & District League since 1903. A tribute to his character and service, this screen was erected by his many friends in 1938.'

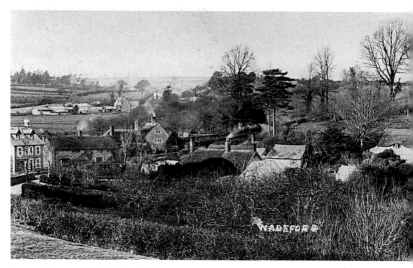

A general view of Wadeford, c. 1900.

Chardstock Rational Club, c. 1908. The club members are gathered in The Square, opposite the George Inn, with the Perry Street Works Band in attendance. Frisby's, of Fore Street, Chard, mentioned on the poster on the left, was one of a chain of such boot and shoe shops throughout the area.

An unknown function in The Square, Chardstock, on 18 April 1909.

Chardstock Cricket Club, c. 1920. Among the players are 'Jolly' Hutchings, Sid Goff, Jack Parris, Albert Goff, Sammy Pearce, Alec Lisle-Smith and Vic Hull the scorer.

Chardstock Cricket Club outside the pavilion at their Burridge Road ground, 1970. From left to right, back row: Stephen Payne, Richard Parris, Pete Bindon, Barry Hutchings, Terry Turner. Front row: Edward Eames, Peter Beviss, Alfie Drewer, Mike Lord, Vivian Eames, Frank Huddy (captain). The Chardstock club was formed in 1887 and played at first on the ground of the closed Chardstock College. They moved to Stony Chilcott in the 1920s and, after the Second World War, to their present home. They celebrated their centenary in 1987 with a well-written history, but their real highlight was a couple of years earlier when the BBC featured the club as a typical village side in their *And it is Chardstock to Bat* programme. Fittingly the game chosen, by accident, was against All Saints, Chardstock's nearest and deadliest rivals.

Right: Annie Hodge's village shop, Chardstock, *c.* 1950. It remained unchanged for over 100 years until it was closed in the 1980s when Mrs Hodge called it a day at the age of ninety-four.

Below: J. Brett's drapers shop opposite the George Inn, Chardstock, 1900. It was one of six shops in the village at the time and Mr Brett, like Annie Hodge, ran the shop into a ripe old age and eventually died in his mid-nineties.

Chardstock General Stores, c. 1969. Formerly the village bakehouse and run by the Miller family, it became a general store in 1959 when it was run by Frank Huddy. By the time of this picture it had been purchased by a Mr and Mrs Woolford but today it is a residential bungalow.

The opening of the new skittle alley at the Tytherleigh Arms in 1955. Among those watching a director of Brutton, Mitchell, Tom's brewery throwing the first ball are Bert Larcombe, Neil Harris, John Newbery, Bob Larcombe, Bill Allen, Donald Goff, Bob Huddy, Ed Larcombe, Ted Pearce and Mrs Smith the landlady.

Chardstock Army Cadet Force, c. 1955.

Chardstock was very much a rural village when this picture was taken in the early 1900s. Here two teams are busy turning hay.

Bringing home the hay in Chardstock, *c.* 1910. Mr Bonfield is working outside his smithy on the left, and, in the background, two of the then five pubs in the village, the Five Bells and the thatched George Inn, stand cheek by jowl.

Acknowledgements

Most of the pictures in this book come from the Jeff Farley collection and we owe him a big thank-you. Other pictures have been lent by Sheila Baker, Gertrude Beasley, Alan Brown, Brian Cooke, Barbara Grabham, Jean Hyde, Helen Meech, Geoff Packer and Christine Webber and we must also thank them all. Some research has been necessary at the offices of the *Chard & Ilminster News* where the staff are always more courteous and helpful than duty demands. The *Chard & Ilminster News* has, of course, faithfully recorded Chard's history since 1855. Thanks must go to Les Berry for his excellent introduction; Les is Chardian born and bred, and now known throughout East Devon as a local historian of much repute. Lastly we appreciate the help of the staff of Nonsuch Publishing, especially David Buxton.

With all Good Wishes from CHARD.